52 QUOTES TO
COLOR YOUR WEEKS

52 QUOTES TO COLOR YOUR WEEKS

...plus a few more

Sally Friedman

Book design by The Troy Book Makers
Printed in the United States of America

The Troy Book Makers • Troy, New York • thetroybookmakers.com

To order additional copies of this title,
contact your favorite local bookstore
or visit www.tbmbooks.com

ISBN: 978-1-61468-291-2

Acknowledgments

Particular thanks go to Doris Friedman, Karyn Kalita, Mandy Moran, Curtis G. Schmitt, Brian White, and Yolanda Williams for their input, their belief in me, and the inspiration they provide. To each of you, I appreciate you.

I would also like to thank Donna Kozik. I haven't officially taken her class, but her program How To Write a Book in a Weekend proved to be the impetus for the current project. What a cool idea to take something that seems impossible (writing a book in a weekend) and to help people turn that dream into a reality.

A reality made all that much clearer through the work of the staff at The Troy Book Makers, who did such a wonderful job of laying this book out on paper.

Finally, it was the inspiration provided by working with Tori Hartman and her deck of Color Wisdom Cards (now the Chakra Oracle Wisdom Cards) that led to the opportunity for me to engage in a round of my own personal growth and the chance to rekindle my long-standing engagement with color.

Thanks, all!

Forward

Here's a little book of 52 quotes (plus a few more) using color as the basis. The purpose—along with the paragraphs of commentary about each—is intended to provide you with some food for thought, to serve as a chance for you to explore and to engage, and as needed, to give you even that little extra ounce of inspiration.

But exactly how "should" you work with this material, and why color? As you will quickly see, there's a lot of open ended material throughout this book. There's no particular organization to the quotes. Not by color. Not by theme. Not by dates during which the authors lived. Even more, as will become clear, this book is full of questions, particularly at the beginning and the end of the commentary following each quote. And most of those questions are pretty open ended, leaving plenty of room for you to use the book in a way that feels right to you.

There are no right or wrong answers. Sometimes, what might pop into your head could connect with something in your life that's really big: what's my next career move? More often, what could resonate with you could come down to something much, much smaller: what kind of ice cream do I want, and how soon can I get it? For me, it's often helpful to start with the small and to realize that even a series of what we think of as "baby steps" may more quickly than we anticipate add up to something much, much bigger.

To facilitate exploration and engagement, I have ended each discussion with two features: a question leading back to the kind of reflection you started at the beginning and a suggestion to take an action step in the course of the week!

Again, not necessarily anything big. Just some step to concretize anything you thought about or learned or got interested in based on what you read. Hey, reading is important, but for many of us, it's specific actions, even small ones, that lead to real growth and change.

In short, there are about as many ways to work with this book as there are colors out there in the universe, and obviously, that means quite a lot!

You might want to be pretty thorough, keeping some sort of journal on your thoughts. You might be moved to find some quiet space and meditate on a quote or a color. You might want to focus on the action steps. As the book's title suggests, the "52" quotes to color your weeks indicates that you might pick up the book by focusing on one quote per week, taking time to reflect, to answer the questions, and to try a couple of specific action steps on the basis of your reflection. Finally, as it moves you, you might simply want to open up to a random page to receive a little inspiration.

However you do it, mostly keep it simple, and mostly just enjoy.

Finally, why color? The answer begins with the personal. From consistently having a box of crayons or construction paper or "go fish" color cards around as a kid, I seem to be drawn to color, the differences between colors, and the impact color has on our lives. Just think about it. Color is all around us. It provides one vehicle for teaching us that there's more abundance—in this case of color—out there than we think. It is one way to help us learn more about who we really are, and color can be just plain fun!

What's your favorite color? Where did that preference come from? Did you say red? Is that because you're passionate, angry, active—to cite some of the stereotypic associations we link to the color red. Did you answer green? Well, you like nature? You need more calm and steadiness in your life? Again, just some of the common associations we link to the color green.

See how much you can get out of/learn from even one simple question about color.

In the end, I hope your take-away after perusing what I think are a pretty cool set of quotes using color—taken from celebrities, athletes, artists, authors, and even a couple of philosophers—genuinely provides a chance for some food for thought, some exploration and engagement, and as needed, even some inspiration.*

---

* Why these particular quotes? Quite simply, after what turned out to be some pretty extensive internet searching, these are the ones that resonated with me, led me to reflect, or even provided good old-fashioned inspiration. There are a lot of quotes out there; these are the ones I liked best.

Perspectives on Disagreement

"Blue is the only color which maintains its own character in all its tones...it will always stay blue; whereas yellow is blackened in its shades, and fades away when lightened; red when darkened becomes brown, and diluted with white is no longer red, but another color—pink."

– Raoul Dufy (artist)

What do you think of this observation? Which color do you identify with here: blue because it remains "true" blue even after being lightened or darkened, or yellow or red, which in fact can be altered by diverse shadings? More, how might you adapt this idea to your relationships and interpersonal conflicts?

In and of themselves, these are interesting facts about color. Metaphorically, they also raise important questions about our connections and communications with others. When you're faced with a conflict or disagreement, how do you handle it? In what ways do you stick to your own side (blue), or do you let your position take on different (red or yellow) shadings, even allowing for the possibility of change and transformation? Under what circumstances do you lean toward one of these positions, or do you in fact operate in a different mode altogether?

Clearly, there are no right answers; just an interesting query with pros and cons and potential caveats on each side.

How do these ideas resonate with you, what connections might you make between your color preferences and your modes of operation in relationships, and what one or two actions might you take this week to put these thoughts into practice?

Enthusiasm

"I fell off my pink cloud with a thud."

– Elizabeth Taylor (actress)

So one minute, you're in a happy place; the world is your stage, and you're totally enjoying the highs of riding on that pink cloud. What activities are you engaging in? Who are you hanging out with? What kinds of thoughts were in your head that were empowering you?

Oops, and then what was that thud about that brought you back down to earth? What happened? What stopped working? What changed?

Elizabeth Taylor's quote raises intriguing questions about the activities we engage in and the things we tell ourselves to get us feeling good or bad. In and of itself, that's worth knowing because the more we consciously shed light on what makes us happy or what brings us down, the more we can take control and the more we can learn to spend time up there in that place pretty close to the clouds.

Perhaps even more importantly, the quote reminds us simply to feel. Whether it's having fun on a pink cloud or thudding back to earth, let's take advantage to get the most we can out of every experience.

As a final note, after you've been brought down, how do you empower yourself to hop back up and quickly search out even more beautiful terrain?

How do these ideas resonate with you, and in what one or two ways this week might you take a couple of actions to make sure you're spending just a little more time on your own happy pink cloud?

Focus on Happiness

"Orange is the happiest color."

– Frank Sinatra (singer)

Do you agree? Is orange the happiest color? Other contenders? Have you given any thought to these questions, and in what ways do they tune us in to thinking about the things that more generally make us feel good?

I like the emphasis on the positive here, and for me, the quote is particularly meaningful because it comes from a singer who is associated with so much talent but who is also renowned for his heartfelt renditions of some very sad love songs. If such a man also put so much stock in happiness, then why not follow his lead. Carry on his illustrious tradition?

How frequently do we do the opposite: highlight the negative, talk about the downside, or over-focus on the pieces of our lives we see as not working?

For me, orange is indeed a happy color. It's bright. It stands out. It highlights uniqueness, and it says, have a good time.

What things make you happy? How can you make it a point to put more attention on them? In what one or two ways this week might you have some fun using "orange"—or for that matter some other color—to trigger your own focus on happiness?

Hey, Frank Sinatra was pretty darned successful. We could do worse than to follow his lead.

And as they say in the city of Syracuse—along with several other happy places across the country—in honor of their teams that have shown so much excellence in sports: Go Orange!

How do these ideas resonate with you, and what one or two actions might you take this week to expand your focus on happiness?

An Unexpected Smile

"If we were to imagine an orange on the blue side or green on the red side or violet on the yellow side, it would give us the same impression as a north wind coming from the southwest."

— *Ludwig Wittgenstein (philosopher)*

What in the world is Wittgenstein talking about?

But at the same time as you ask, perhaps you decide you're not really interested in any extended explanation. You would just like to enjoy the colorful imagery and the goofiness of the juxtaposition of compass directions that focus you simultaneously on traveling "north" and "southwest." You simply want to have the experience of taking in an observation that highlights the playfulness of an author who is clearly having fun.

If we do wish to speculate as to his underlying logic, perhaps Wittgenstein is emphasizing connections between things that are already related as well as the attraction or transformation of opposites. Pairs of blue and orange, red and green, and yellow and violet are after all complementary colors 180 degrees apart on the color wheel, and north and southwest are (sort of) across from each other on a compass.

Alternatively, as a constructivist philosopher who liked to draw associations between disparate ideas, maybe Wittgenstein wanted to make some profound metaphysical linkage between color and compass directions. Or perhaps he wanted to encourage us to develop our own imaginations, and maybe coming up with a "silly" observation was his way of showing us how that might be done.

Regardless, there is no question we could productively approach this quote from an intellectual perspective. We could take the time to understand the context that motivated his writing, and we could try to figure out whether or not he was saying something philosophical or important. For now, it seems more enjoyable to move things in a much simpler direction. It's more fun to enjoy his imagery and his creativity, to savor a colorful moment, and to just smile.

How do these ideas resonate with you, what one or two experiences this week made you smile, and what couple of actions could you take to insure that the smiles keep coming?

You!

"The white light streams down to be broken up by those human prisms into all the colors of the rainbow. Take your own color in the pattern and be just that.

– H. Jackson Brown, Jr. *(author)*

As H. Jackson Brown points out, here's an interesting fact you might remember from high school physics. White light can be broken up—through a prism—into a rainbow of all the colors of the spectrum.

A pretty cool idea, isn't it: that there's so much going on and so many hidden colors just waiting to pop out from what we thought was clear white light.

And the process can work the other way as well. If we combine all the spectrum colors, we get white—an obviously different color from its component parts.

By extension, what if we apply these ideas to how we think about each other? After all, each one of us can be considered on the one hand holistically, or on the other hand as someone who has many, many preferences, feelings, interests, etc. I'm Sally, but I also like to walk (green), have a dog (tan), get angry (red), and am pretty loyal (blue). At the same time, there's a whole to me that goes deeper than my specific characteristics and preferences. I like colors, walk every day, and enjoy writing, but there's of course more to me than each of those qualities considered separately. I'm Sally!

Sometimes I want to highlight a part; sometimes it's better to focus on the whole.

All important ideas well worth consideration.

And there's actually another point that H. Jackson Brown wants to make too. He would like each of us to see the prism in another light entirely: to help get us thinking about what's most important to us and about who we really are. Of all the colors of the rainbow refracted from that prism, what's your favorite? What does that color reflect about you? How might it symbolize one of your important strengths or some piece of you that you want to get a little more out there in the world?

How do these ideas resonate with you, and what are one or two actions you could take this week to be just a little bit truer to who you really are?

One Small Act

"There are painters who transform the sun to a yellow spot, but there are others who, with the help of their art and their intelligence, transfer a yellow spot into the sun."

– *Pablo Picasso (artist)*

What a powerful idea: to start with something small and seemingly insignificant—a yellow spot on a canvas—and to transform it into something meaningful and wonderful—an image of the sun.

You never know what might come out of just starting!

With this quote, Picasso, who should know, has gone one step further to provide a recipe—at least one that worked for him—for bringing this kind of transformation to fruition. It takes, as he says, a combination of art and intelligence.

Now, I don't think you have to be a great artist to appreciate the power of these words. Instead, how do they apply to your own experience? What "small" action have you taken in the past that has led to something much bigger or contributed to the betterment of a situation in an important way? What set of circumstances, on your end and perhaps with the support of others, helped bring about this transformation, and what's your own recipe for success when you want to make a change?

I like the idea that a series of small actions—sometimes even just one such action—can set in motion a chain of events leading to an outcome of much greater significance. You don't have to begin a transformation with a bang!

Even more, I am inspired by the sense of agency and empowerment. I might not be a great painter with the "art and intelligence" to produce a visual image to inspire the "masses." But I can certainly come up with ways I can transform some "yellow spot" to make a big difference in my life, even creating a wonderful, happier sun.

How do these ideas resonate with you, and in what one or two ways this week might you find inspiration from Picasso's words to take a small step toward creating something better in your own life?

Celebrating Difference

"How wonderful yellow is. It stands for the sun."

– *Vincent Van Gogh (artist)*

"What a horrible thing yellow is."

– *Edgar Degas (artist)*

Hmm, perhaps a difference of opinion here? Do you get the idea that these two individuals, both famous painters from the middle to late 1800s, don't see eye to eye on this? Do you get the idea that Van Gogh likely used a lot more yellow in his paintings?

Neither exactly minces words!

So, how do you yourself see the color yellow?

And since there's clearly a difference of opinion here, how do you in your turn deal with disagreement? In what ways do you shove it under the rug? Start arguing and take a side? Do you think of the "other guy" as an opponent, or do you attempt to understand his or her perspective? Do you see differences of opinion as a normal and natural part of life, or are they really hard for you to handle?

For many of us, including me, conflict and difference can be a tough one, and there are obviously many perspectives on how to deal with them.

But maybe there's a lesson here from the views of these two great artists as well as from the art world more generally. After all, art is a place where different opinions and perspectives are not only expected, but they're also accepted. Some people like certain paintings, movies or music, and others don't. It's as simple as that. No need to convince others they're right or wrong. No need to shove conflict and differ-ence under the rug. It comes down to taste, and as a natural part of the entertainment experience, it's all pretty normal.

How do these ideas resonate with you? With respect to the color yellow in particular, do you lean more to the Degas or the Van Gogh end of the spectrum, and with respect to conflict and differences more generally, in what one or two ways this week might you apply these ideas to make a situa-tion in your life better?

A Matter of Perspective

"I cannot pretend to feel impartial about colors. I rejoice with the brilliant ones and am genuinely sorry for the poor browns."

– *Winston Churchill (Prime Minister of England)*

"The color brown, I realized, is anything but nondescript. It comes in as many hues as there are colors of earth, which is commonly presumed infinite."

– *Barbara Kingsolver (author, from Animal Dreams)*

Wow, can you imagine two more different opinions about the color brown? The first—let's call it the dull view—comes from Winston Churchill, in his own right actually a pretty good painter. Contrast the perspective—call it the variety view—of well-known author Barbara Kingsolver.

There's no right or wrong here. Some people like the color brown; others don't. What's more relevant is to appreciate first of all that each of us is in fact operating from a perspective—be it about colors or money or relationships—and to make those perspectives more a part of our conscious thinking. Are we coming from a standpoint that currently works for us, or are we stuck in an outmoded view of things?

From there, let's acknowledge that different people, even people we may care about a lot, may be seeing things from very different world views than our own. How helpful might it be to bring to light these differences, with the potential to further dialogue and understanding?

I have to say in this case I'd like to think I'm looking at the world more from the Kingsolver side than that of Churchill, but that of course, is my own viewpoint.

How do these ideas resonate with you, what view do you have about the color brown, and in what one or two ways this week could you apply ideas about perspective to a situation in your own life?

Love in Action

"Love is like a rainbow, where each color will flow. Red, of the heart that beats. Orange, funny and sweet. Yellow, warm rays of sun. Green, having lots of fun. Blue, waves of sky above. Purple, the color of love. With each color comes a nice smile; hearts are beating at a thousand miles.

– Anonymous

What do you think? What color do you relate to most here, or is it the overall image of a rainbow that most appeals to you? More, what do these lines suggest to you about ways you might add a little more love to your life?

The quote above adds a lighthearted twist and provides a different perspective on how we might view what can become some pretty challenging situations. For example, when I myself think of putting a little more love out there, the first thing that comes to mind is that it's going to be difficult. There's the work of developing stronger communication skills, the inherent uncertainty of taking the risks to meet new people, and the understandable concern about whether others will like you.

Hmm, might as well back off and spend more time alone!

But what if it's not really so hard, and what if it's not all about "work"? What if it's more about capturing the fun and light and joy of the beautiful rainbow and taking advantage of the qualities we associate with each of its wonderful colors? Hey, let's get out there and put into action some of the associations we have with the colors. Let's engage in some activities that incorporate some of the "funny and sweet" of orange," the "warm rays" of a yellow sun, and certainly the "lots of fun" invoked by green. Let's wear the red or the blue or the purple to remind us that at bottom it's about being lighthearted, and let's use the image of the rainbow to focus on the things that are just good.

Each color contributes its own character to the mix while at the same time the totality of the rainbow opens up and expands some pretty exciting possibilities.

How do these ideas resonate with you, and what are one or two things you could do this week to more actively put a little more rainbow love out into the universe?

The Most Important Thing /
The Heart of the Matter

"When you photograph people in color, you photograph their clothes. But when you photograph people in black and white, you photograph their souls!"

– Ted Grant (photographer, author)

As the "color reading professor," I'm not sure I exactly agree with this, but I sure get the point. When do you get distracted by the frivolous or the superficial—what photographer Ted Grant labels "color"—and when are you more likely to get to the black-and-white heart of the matter? Do you sometimes concentrate on what's on the surface to avoid the essence of the "truth"?

It's not always a bad thing to focus on the so-called "trivial," and indeed, sometimes such a mindset can have surprising benefits. For instance, maybe Mr. Grant is downplaying the possibility that some of the things—having a nice wardrobe—that we too easily write off as superficial really serve as a signal to let go a little in the name of some good old-fashioned fun. Additionally, as you listen to people's conversations, sometimes it takes a certain amount of "fluff" or "processing" to get to what really is the heart of the matter. And sometimes getting to the heart of the matter can take considerable effort.

But at the same time, as Mr. Grant identifies, too much color/fluff can often be distracting. We get sidetracked by what's easy to see. We pay too much attention to people's clothes, people's looks, and things that we assess as just plain pretty.

So cutting through any extra "color," let's put more focus on things that truly matter. What remains as black and white? What stands out as distinct or fundamental? What's the "true" thing you really want to say, highlight, or take action on? Finally, what is needed to help you develop clearer answers to these questions, and once you've got those knowings, how might you move forward, even bringing more color into the process?

How do these ideas resonate with you, and what are one or two things you could do this week to cut through the "color" to get closer to the heart of a matter important to you?

A Good Attitude

"Gray skies are just clouds passing over."

– Duke Ellington (musician)

You agree, right? We have all seen some gray skies/ have had some not so happy experiences. Something didn't work out the way you thought it would, or you just had a proverbial "gray" day.

First off, as is true of the positivity associated with gazing up at the sky to enjoy its blueness and the wonders of nature, these "negative" gray experiences are natural and normal— no reflection on any great scheme for the way we're handling our lives. Nor do we need to see ourselves (as we often do) as "bad" or "wrong" just because there are some bumps in the road or some gray in the moment.

Second, though Duke doesn't phrase it this way, it might be worth traveling deeper into the clouds in those darker skies. What do you learn from things that didn't turn out the way you wanted? Perhaps the feelings in those gray clouds need to be expressed? And once those emotions are out in the open, what's the take-away, and what's the next step towards lessening the "grayness"?

We tend to complicate things. We turn those bumps in the road into mountains too difficult to climb. But hey, it's a simple quote. So let's keep the thought simple too. "Gray skies are just clouds passing over." It doesn't take much to return to a natural brilliant blue.

How do these ideas resonate with you, and in what one or two ways this week might you acknowledge some "grayness," and then move on?

Attitude

"Your attitude is like a box of crayons that color your world. Constantly color your picture gray, and your picture will always be bleak. Try adding some bright colors to the picture by including humor, and your picture begins to lighten up."

– Allen Klein (author, motivational speaker, humorist)

Are you someone who takes things pretty seriously, or do you like to have fun? Do you tend to view the glass as half full, or are you likely to see it as heading toward empty? Does your attitude vary with the setting? How likely are you in the first place to notice the mindset with which you're walking around?

I like this quote because it highlights the importance of attitude. Not circumstance. Not action. Just plain attitude!

So with what kind of standpoint do you generally approach the world? Like the colors in a box of crayons, there are many perspectives you can bring to bear on any situation, and the quote suggests you have more conscious choice about which one you can choose at any given moment than you might think. You can obviously feel positively or negatively about something—optimistic or pessimistic. You can walk around with a lot of confidence, or you can choose to hold back. You can take note of the intensity of your feelings, and of course, your attitude can fluctuate depending on what's going on around you.

As examples, there's the perspective of confidence you see in an athlete secure in her abilities compared to the standpoint of the hesitant child too timid to take risks.

There's the person with the genuinely sunny disposition who can put a positive spin on even the worst situation, or the pessimist who is sure things will never go right.

The imagery of a box of crayons is so evocative because it gets us thinking not only about just how many different ways there are to view your experience but also how many different choices you have as to which perspective to adopt. You're viewing a situation through a blue lens; what would it look like if you pulled out a red crayon? You're seeing something in terms of black and white; what might be different if you switched those colors to yellow and orange? Things appear to be pretty black; what if you added just a little white?

And it is the lightness of that white that brings us back to the original point of Mr. Klein's quote. Of all the various possibilities out there, how often do you choose a perspective emphasizing "humor"? Under what conditions can you take things less personally, remember to ease up, or just plain make a conscious effort to inject a little more fun?

So it's not always about taking action. Attitude matters too, and cultivating a positive one may yield more benefits than you might think.

How do these ideas resonate with you, and what are one or two things you could do this week to make sure you're walking around with just a little more of a fun attitude?

Embracing the New?

"Color television! Bah, I won't believe it until I see it in black and white."

— Samuel Goldwyn (Hollywood executive/producer)

What is Goldwyn saying here? In his view, it's better to see things in black and white than in many shades and colors. As he sees it, contrast, simplicity, and clarity are more valuable than variety, shadings, and nuance. Interesting ideas to consider, right?

Let's not lose this query too easily.

But let's also consider the larger implications from this particular speaker. Goldwyn was a movie pioneer/executive whose fifty-year career dated approximately from World War I through the late 1950s. He thus saw the film industry transformed from silent films to talkies and from black and white (his own stock and trade) to early developments in color.

While I don't know the context for this quote—was he embracing the transformation to color, hence expressing tongue and cheek, or was he being serious—his quote does raise critical questions about when and how to affirm the new. Think about your own attitude towards the modern day version of the kinds of technological changes on which Goldwyn focused. For example, have you become expert at searching on Google, or do you still seek out the card catalog at your local library? Are your Facebook settings consistently set to "on" or do you "abhor" the possibility of a live chat? Do you get the most out of LinkedIn or Pinterest, or would you rather just pick up an old-fashioned phone?

And of course, technological transformation, as consequential as it has been as we head further into the information age, is only the tip of the change iceberg. How do you deal with the myriad of other transitions? Starting a new relationship? Moving to another city? The closing of your favorite bookstore?

Under what circumstances do you embrace the new, wholeheartedly jumping on the bandwagon of innovation? When do you hold back, relying on tried and true habits, routines, or standard operating procedures, and how often in the first place do you even think about how you handle change?

With the hindsight of over 50 years, Goldwyn's particular views about the virtues of black and white over color may have some merit but mostly seem rather amusing. The broader questions his quote raises will remain relevant throughout time.

How do these ideas resonate with you, and in what one or two ways this week might you take some action to deal with a change in a way that truly feels right for you?

Disappointment / Dissatisfaction

"The people who live in a golden age usually go around complaining how yellow everything looks."

– Randall Jarrell (poet, novelist)

How do you handle disappointment? What do you do when things don't live up to your expectations? When they turn into what appear to be not very positive directions?

These are hard questions because disappointment can hurt—sometimes a lot.

Randall Jarrell's quote speaks to a certain kind of disappointment, the kind where you're comparing some apparently glorious past to a supposedly not as wonderful present. If you think about it, he's right. You hear a lot of talk about what we refer to as golden ages: in entertainment, in transportation, and according to some, even in the greatness of U.S. civilization. At a more personal level, many of us look to particular times in our lives when we felt happiest, perhaps thinking we'll never again find so much joy.

It's not hard to apply the same logic to any number of other circumstances, and it's pretty easy to see things as "yellow" when you really want them to bring "gold."

But how do you handle these situations? How do you get past getting stuck in what Randall Jarrell is describing as "yellow"? In what ways do you either meld that yellow into an alloy that feels closer to the proverbial gold; or instead, what needs to happen to help you come to decide that perhaps the yellow gives you a pretty good life in its own right? How do you get to a place where—be it yellow, gold, or any other color—you appreciate that it's all really good?

How do these ideas resonate with you, and what this week are one or two things you could do to turn a disappointment even into an opportunity?

Roots

"My fondest hope is that Roots *may start black, white, brown, red, yellow people digging back for their own roots. Man, that would make me feel 90 feet tall."*

– Alex Haley (author)

How much have you thought about the circumstances under which you were raised or the impact of these roots on your current life? What do you know about how your parents, grandparents or even family members of prior generations grew up, and what kind of imprints have they left on you?

In the 1970s, Alex Haley's novel (later a television mini-series) *Roots* captured the attention of our nation. The compelling characters—including Kunta Kinte and Chicken George, to mention only a few—represented by successive generations of Haley's family were of social significance as an important recognition of the telling of the history of African-Americans in the United States.[*] More generally, the work was influential in pointing people of all races and backgrounds towards exploring genealogy and finding out more about their ancestors.

Haley really helped people get curious. Where did your grandfather come from? His father? Perhaps his father before him? What were they like? How did they live?

---

[*] The stellar cast of the mini-series serves as another indicator of the influence of the project. The list of distinguished actors includes but is by no means limited to the following Hollywood luminaries: Ben Vereen, LeVar Burton, Leslie Uggams, Cicely Tyson, Chuck Connors, Edward Asner, Lloyd Bridges, Lorne Greene, and many more.

Fast-forwarding into the present, even more intriguing questions arise. In what ways does an emphasis on roots help us operate with more understanding and clarity in the current day? When and how does something from the past, however distant, become relevant, and how do we handle it? When do we delve into a deeper understanding of long ago events, or alternatively, under what conditions do we say to ourselves, "Yes, prior circumstances play a role, but the past is in the past. What do I do now?"

Haley's work suggests that exploring our roots can have a greater impact on the present than we might expect.

How do these ideas resonate with you, in what one or two ways this week might family heritage be relevant in your life, and what's one action you could take based on that understanding?

Light

"I really just want to be warm yellow light that pours over everyone I love."

— *Conor Oberst (singer/songwriter)*

Hmm, in what ways this week has your own warm yellow light "poured" over people you love? How much thought have you given to this? How have you made a conscious effort to make sure it happens?

These are actually pretty profound questions.

How have you lent a hand, included others in your plans, or simply remembered to speak a word of support? Considered someone else's viewpoint or perspective? Acted in service in a conscious way?

Sounds somewhat daunting, doesn't it? Sometimes the idea of reaching out to others at least for me raises the fear that I won't get my own needs met? That I'll lose my own focus?

Yet, the idea of the quote speaks of warmth, light, and love, and it opens up new possibilities. Instead of seeing stretching to help others as a burden, what if we more often came to view love in the best sense? Hey come on, don't we want to do good things, say kind words, and generally make things better for the people closest to us? What about creating more win-wins? And even more, if what's involved is simply "pouring" warm yellow light, what if it's easier than we think to send out the kindness, the warmth, and the genuine affection?

How do these ideas resonate with you, and in what one or two ways this week might you choose to spread your own warm yellow light?

Camaraderie

"Toad talked big about all he was going to do in the days to come, while stars grew fuller and larger all around them, and a yellow moon, appearing suddenly and silently from nowhere in particular, came to keep them company and listen to their talk."

— Kenneth Grahame (author,
from The Wind in the Willows*)*

Do you remember back when you were a kid and you were so proud you could stay up all night? Listening to music by yourself or just enjoying the company of a friend? As you got older, there were those slumber parties alive with girl (or boy) talk, camping trips where you told stories around a fire, or just times when you could hang with people you liked, exploring your plans for the future and reveling in the certainty that things would work out. Being out in nature, at least for me, has the potential to enrich the quality of these experiences.

Powerful moments long remembered.

So with the blessing of the stars and the bright yellow moon, Toad and his friends from the classic *The Wind in the Willows* got to do these things, to share feelings of closeness, and to simply develop their dreams.

Kenneth Grahame evokes some eloquent imagery here. Any one of the elements he describes—the friendships and support, the meandering conversations, the exploration of hopes, the life of the outdoors—are enough to hook me in. In combination, these elements bring back some pretty great childhood memories, and more importantly, they help set out a vision of some pieces I want more of in my current adult life.

How do these ideas resonate with you, and what are one or two things you could do this week, perhaps underneath a literal or metaphorical yellow moon, to rekindle some important piece of this picture?

Loyalty

"I bleed Dodger blue and when I die, I'm going to the big Dodger in the sky."

— Tommy Lasorda (baseball man)

What do you really care about? What are the one or two things in your life which most define you? What would need to happen for you to get clear on some answers here, and in what ways might such clarity be beneficial?

The long time former manager of the Los Angeles baseball team doesn't seem to need to engage in such reflection. His allegiances and loyalties are clear. Tommy Lasorda knows what he cares about, he's sure of his place, he's enthusiastic, and he's loyal to the cause. No ambiguity about what he stands for or what's first and foremost in his heart.

Do you wonder if he's exaggerating just a tad?

But how cool is it to be such a fan and to have such enthusiasm! To be so sure of what matters to you that you'll even bet that your loyalty is shared by the "Big Dodger in the sky."

Of course, there are some tradeoffs to being so partisan. How do you put up with things when your side is doing badly? Can you really acknowledge when they're just plain wrong? What about any need to compromise? Even admitting that the Yankees might be doing a good job?

And yet, what a wonderful thing to have such a sense of certainty, loyalty, and belonging.

How do these ideas resonate with you? In what ways this week might you get a little clearer on your own loyalties, and if you like, what are one or two things you could do to enhance the bonds?

Stepping Out!

"I think I have something tonight that's not quite correct for evening wear... blue suede shoes."

– Elvis Presley (singer)

What are some ways you have gone against the grain to do something that wasn't exactly socially correct? Engaged in some activity folks close to you might disapprove of? Stepped out in the face of some risk to put your true self out there?

Okay, so let's set the context. The quote is from Elvis Presley, the all-time king of rock 'n' roll, who likely could wear just about anything he wanted to any social occasion.

And okay, for Elvis, wearing blue suede shoes to a party has a special significance. After all, years later, that remains one of his most beloved songs. Anyone would be thrilled if Elvis came to a party wearing his blue suede shoes.

Yet, at a deeper level, the quote has more to say than even Elvis might have intended. Whether it's the clothes we wear to a social event, the conversations we have with friends, or our general attitude towards taking risks, how we choose to balance the need to conform with the need to put our true self front and center says a lot about who we are.

There are of course solid reasons for hesitating to step out. There's the desire we all have to fit in, the ease and safety of conforming, and the natural inclination to please others. Sometimes we just don't want to make waves. But hey, maybe it's worth just one shot at bringing those blue suede shoes to a black tie party, and maybe the dancing will prove easier than you expect.

How do these ideas resonate with you, and what this week are one or two things you could do to get out those blue suede shoes and take them to an unexpected place?

Novelty

"Every time I walk down one of those red carpets, you think I'd be used to it after all these years, but it's like it's happening for the first time."

— *Jeff Bridges (actor)*

What a wonderful way to approach the world. The imagery of the red carpet, as well as all the perks we associate with it, doesn't need to be confined to our treatment of celebrities. What if we gave more thought to extending some of that treatment to the friends and neighbors so much a part of our lives? Even towards ourselves? What if we more often approached life with the attitude that each of us is special, therefore deserving of nothing but the best? An inspiring perspective to cultivate and one to energize others.

And what about the approach Jeff Bridges takes to his circumstances? As an award winning actor, he certainly has journeyed along that red carpet many, many times. Does it get old for him? Does he get bored? Does he say, "Same thing, different day"? Not hardly.

Don't you get the idea he's enjoying each occasion to the max and getting the max out of each occasion?

He's looking at each experience through fresh eyes and appreciating and valuing it for its own unique character. Extrapolating, he's reveling in the novelty, learning new things, and just plain living in the moment.

How do these ideas resonate with you, and in what one or two ways this week might you apply this kind of "fresh eyes" perspective to a task you have engaged in many, many times?

Experiment

"I don't wear bright orange clothes or leopard skin boots, but it was really good fun to play someone that does and have an excuse to!"

— *Sally Hawkins (actress)*

Can you think of some times when you have tried something you never thought you'd do? Worn clothes you thought didn't reflect your style? Gone to a beach even though you preferred the mountains or vice versa? Checked out a book that you thought wouldn't be your taste?

How did you feel about such experiences? Resist them strongly? Enjoy the novelty? Other?

Sally Hawkins clearly enjoys trying new things, and her energy is contagious, pushing me towards wanting to engage in a little experimentation of my own. It's probably true that her profession as an actress puts her in a position to experiment with more roles and to see what it feels like to play different characters than many of the rest of us. Yet she's pretty persuasive, pointing us in new directions and reminding us this kind of engagement can be surprisingly fun. You don't like flamboyance? Put on a little orange to see how it feels. You are drawn to wearing some really bright colors; what would it be like to check out some dark brown?

At least from my own perspective, I'm naturally hesitant to engage in things I am pretty sure I won't like, and I'm likely to evaluate how an experience is going even before it has actually ended. But if you see engaging in new things as simply trying out roles that are different for you, rather than as experiences you feel compelled to enjoy, the perspective changes to something quite different. What can be learned?

How can you broaden your horizons? What point of view can you better understand?

Perhaps, as it has been for Sally Hawkins, maybe trying out some new roles can even turn out to be just plain fun.

How do these ideas resonate with you? How this week, even in one or two small ways, might you get past that natural tendency to resist what's different for you, to do something out of character, or to take on an unfamiliar role?

Hidden Treasures

"White... is not a mere absence of colour; it is a shining and affirmative thing, as fierce as red, as definite as black... God paints in many colours; but He never paints so gorgeously, I had almost said so gaudily, as when He paints in white."

– *Gilbert K. Chesterton* (*author*)

Can you think of a time when you walked past something only to, upon instinct, retrace your steps and find value? Have you had the experience of coming to realize that the few words spoken by a quiet person can carry as much weight as the many of someone more outspoken? What about the experience of focusing on someone's glitzy clothes only to discover the friend in jeans walking beside her was actually more interesting?

I don't mean to stereotype. A tendency to talk frequently has no necessary correlation with the quality of your speech. Nor does the nature of your dress connect to the substance of your character.

But how much of the time, rightly or wrongly, do we pay more attention to people, things, or places that are "easy" for us to notice? How often do we not give a second look to find more interesting aspects of a situation? For that matter, when do we even give thought to which pieces of an experience we are actually attending to?

As Chesterton's view of the color white reminds us, there's no need to be "as fierce as red" or "as definite as black" to make a contribution.

So what if instead we more often approached life with a different mindset, looking for the hidden treasures in the things we're less likely to notice? What if we even made it our own little game? After all, you never know what will come out of keener observation. The neutral and less flashy "white... is not a mere absence of colour; it is a shining and affirmative thing."

How do these ideas resonate with you, and how this week might you find one or two ways to practice this kind of keener observation?

Exploration

"Be like Curious George, start with a question and look under the yellow hat to find what's there."

– James Collins (author, researcher, business consultant)

What's one goal or intention that's important to you, and what are some steps you might take to go about achieving said goal? As well, what's something you're just curious about so you simply want to know more? We don't always ask ourselves these sorts of questions.

Enter Curious George, the monkey, and his friend, the man with the yellow hat. From an original set of books, the series expanded to television and movies, and it continues in various forms even to the present day. And to say that George is inquisitive is an understatement; the monkey's curiosity has led him into all sorts of adventures as he has tagged along on a number of camping trips, has attempted to fly a kite, and has even tried to hold down a job.

While without doubt George's impulsiveness has led him into his fair share of mishaps, it is also true that the spirit of adventure he embodies is very much worth emulating. Get curious. Ask questions. What might I try that I haven't before? What if I took a different route to work? What couple of things could I do to make my day go easier? The possibilities for things to ask are endless, and often just phrasing things in the form of a question can generate a wider range of options.

Thereafter, it's not just about looking for the quick or easy answer. Still following Curious George, you don't just go with the first idea that pops into your head. Instead, you get the experience of exploring alternatives, possibilities, and choices. I like how Mr. Collins puts it; "look under the yellow hat to find what's there." It's a hat so there's a world of hidden treasures underneath. It's about "finding what's there" so it's true exploration, reflection, and intuition. And it's the color yellow which traditionally is associated with optimism, cheerfulness, and possibility.

Doesn't the imagery transform what often seems a daunting process into something that even feels fun?

A well-known researcher into the causes of business success, James Collins himself has more than once invoked the image of Curious George to encourage thinking about leadership.

What about you? How this week do these ideas resonate with you, and in what specific one or two ways might you put them into practice?

A Social Context?

"Designers want me to dress like Spring, in billowing things. I don't feel like Spring. I feel like a warm red Autumn."

— Marilyn Monroe (actress)

What's your reaction to Marilyn's predicament? She's being asked to wear clothes and colors she doesn't want to? How important is the issue of appearance? Trivial enough that she's misplacing her focus on superficial things? Important because it involves fundamental choices about how she presents herself and her image to the world?

As an actress of the 1940s and 1950s, Marilyn worked at a time when the studio executives were kings; those entertainment moguls, in ways big and small, had the power to make or break careers. Do we feel sorry for Marilyn because she was stuck in a box of powerlessness, forced to know every whim of every last clothing designer? On the other hand, in light of her own unique star power and status, did she have sufficient cachet to, in her own right, buck the moguls and to set any fashion trends she chose?

Her simple expression of upset raises more questions than she realized. What's most important? What's worth going along with, and when is it worth risking raising some hackles to go against the grain? These issues are faced by each and every one of us in smaller and bigger ways. What particularly stands out for me about Marilyn's case is the social setting of her dilemma. It's the context of an icon in an era of the demands of the great studios in an already demanding industry, and it's the story of a female actress working in a then male dominated field. Whose side would you take? How would you react here?

How do these ideas resonate with you? What are one or two actions you could take this week to follow up on this resonance, and how if at all, does the color red—part of Marilyn's questioning here—add to the intriguing nature of the story?

Anger

"A cat's rage is beautiful, burning with pure cat flame, all its hair standing up and crackling blue sparks, eyes blazing and sputtering."

— *William S. Burroughs (author)*

How do you feel about getting angry? When is the last time, or can you even think of an instance, when you got really upset about something and were happy to acknowledge your feelings? How did you actually decide to express what you wanted to say? How have people important in your life dealt with any situations over which you had strong disagreements?

Mr. Burroughs' quote is so great because it stands as such a contradiction to social taboos about the emotion of anger. Directly and at a less conscious level, we're told a lot of things about anger, but I don't think encouraging its acknowledgment or its expression are the first reactions that come to mind. The messages instead push in the direction of conflict avoidance. We are told to make nice, to sweep conflict under the rug, and at all costs to come to see the other guy's point of view. As males, we are written off as "angry young men" in need of counseling. As females, we are made to feel guilty of "unladylike behavior." In any case, people can get pretty uncomfortable when a person who is angry in the moment "makes a scene."

Against the background of these social taboos, Mr. Burroughs has provided us with such an affirmative description of an emotion we do everything we humans can to shy away from.

So while I don't know much about—and actually am allergic to—the species feline, I sure love hearing about "blue sparks" crackling, "eyes blazing," and "hair standing up" in the context of beauty. How cool is it to have your anger validated! How great to connect your validation with the language of the color blue, which is usually thought of as providing such a soothing and calming context. Hey, if it's okay to get angry even when the environment around you encourages calm, isn't that a way to set the stage for the normalcy of this so-called "negative" emotion?

And if "a cat's rage" can be "beautiful," why can't the same be said for that of a human?

How do these ideas resonate with you, how this week might you transfer any learning from the blue sparks coloring the rage of an angry cat to events in your own life, and what are one or two actions you might take on that basis?

Yes!

"I thank you God for this most amazing day, for the leaping greenly spirits of trees, and for the blue dream of sky and for everything which is natural, which is infinite, which is yes."

– E.E. Cummings (poet)

What are four or five things you have really felt happy about this week? Activities you have engaged in? People you have hung out with? Times you have spent around the house just relaxing?

We find a lot of ways to identify negativity in our lives. Some of this focus makes good sense and can prove helpful in bettering our situation.

What would it be like if we more often countered this perspective by seeing the world from a positive vantage point? What if we asked more questions about what's going right? What's just really good? What's happy?

So, in contrast to some of the usual patterns of negativity, doesn't E.E. Cummings' observation just make you feel good? What's better than being out in nature checking out the green trees and blue skies? What's more affirming than thinking and rethinking times that are so good you really feel close to the "Infinite"? And what's more wonderful than approaching life with the attitude that just says "Yes!"

How do these ideas resonate with you, and what are one or two things you could do this week to bring more "yes" into your life?

Growth

"When you're green, you're growing. When you're ripe, you rot."

– *Ray Kroc (entrepreneur/businessman)*

What do you think? What's your reaction?

This quote really got me smiling.

I get the part about green and growing, but the part about ripe and rot is downright funny. In fact, if I didn't like hamburger joints so much, I could come away from this with some flip comment about who the heck is Ray Kroc, founder of the ultimate fast food chain of McDonald's, to be talking to me about ripening and rotting?

As well, if you take the time to think just a little more deeply, these few words express a surprising amount of wisdom. The most common color in nature, green, does of course symbolize physical growth. Growth of grass, growth of trees, and growth of all things living on the earth. There is likewise, of course, the importance of our psychological and spiritual development.

But there's personal growth, and then there's personal growth. There's a passive kind: When something bad happens, I'll try to process it and learn from the experience. But it probably wasn't my fault anyway, and I really don't want to put that much effort into changing my modus operandi. So sure, I'll do some work on myself, but I'd rather have someone else do the bulk.

In contrast, Ray Crock's view is so wise because it sets personal development front and center as a value to actively pursue. Maybe his imagery of the threat of decay puts a bit too much emphasis on the proverbial stick rather than offering us the carrot of some solid reasons why growth matters; but as he says, it's really pretty simple. If you're green, you're growing. If you're ripe, you're not taking time to grow, and to put it bluntly, therefore you'll rot.

And in the long run, who really wants to live in that kind of rotten camp?

What's your take on Ray Crock's observation, and what one or two things this week have you done to ensure you're engaging in just a little bit of your own personal growing.

"[Orange] is one of God's favorite colors—He stuck it right there between red and yellow as the second color in the rainbow. He decorates entire forests with shades of orange every autumn. It shows up in sunrises at the start of the day, sunsets at the end of the day, and in the glow of the moon at the right time of night."

— *Reggie Joiner (author, from* Think Orange:
Imagine the Impact When Church and Family Collide*)*

What's the first color that comes to mind when you think of the colors you see in nature? The green of grass and trees? The blue of the oceans or the sky? Gray clouds on a rainy day?

I'm betting your first answer here does not reference the color orange! And I bet if you thought about it more, you would have said the appearance of the color orange is actually pretty rare, especially as it shows up in the natural world.

Apparently, wrong!

I like Reggie Joiner's observation. I have no idea what God's favorite color is—I would hope He (or She) likes color in the first place, and I guess She (or He) is entitled to have favorites. Because it's happy and eye catching and because it's a color I like, I also hope Reggie Joiner is right that God has a preference for orange!

Nonetheless, more to the point, Reggie sends out a great reminder that there's more orange out there in the natural world than we might have guessed. Notice those sunrises and sunsets and even changes in the color of the sun at varying times of the day. Take a walk through fall foliage to revel in some wonderful shades, or head outside at night to notice the varying colors of the moon.

And once you start thinking about it, that's only the beginning. What about some especially lovely flowers? Orange trees? Orange markings on some birds? Fruits? Vegetables? Other?

And as well, there's what Reggie also reminds us, the inimitable array of colors so present at times when we're lucky enough to see the totality of the color spectrum in a rainbow. Pretty amazing if you put your mind to it how many surprising things you can first observe and then enjoy.

How do these ideas resonate with you, how might you take time this week to notice more orange or another color of your choice, and more generally, what are one or two things you might try to simply "see" more?

Imagine!

"The bird swam swiftly and gracefully toward the Magic Isle, and as it drew nearer its gorgeously colored plumage astonished them. The feathers were of many hues of glistening greens and blues and purples, and it had a yellow head with a red plume, and pink, white and violet in its tail."

– L. Frank Baum (*author, from* The Magic of Oz)

Hmm, what could we come up with if we just took a little more time to unwind, to recharge and to dream? What if we made it a point to clear space in our schedules to chill, to hang out with ourselves, and to explore whatever comes to mind? To use that space and time to open to new options and possibilities?

How fanciful would you get? Would you come up with, as Baum did, a fictional bird of many colors? A magic carpet that could get you across the universe at the speed of light? A time travel contraption that would let you experience life at different stages of history?

Or would you use the time to be more practical? To plan better options for the next family trip? To think of more intimate dates with your lover? To get clearer about your hopes and dreams for the next few years?

Doesn't Baum's imagery of such a colorful bird get your creative juices flowing, encourage you to have some fun with your imagination, and just plain make you feel happy?

How do these ideas resonate with you, and in what one or two ways this week might you incorporate the spirit of that colorful imaginary bird into your life to use it to generate a few new options, choices, or possibilities?

Neutral Observer

"It suddenly struck me that that tiny pea, pretty and blue, was the Earth. I put up my thumb and shut one eye, and my thumb blotted out the planet Earth. I didn't feel like a giant. I felt very, very small."

– *Neil Armstrong (astronaut)*

What do you think? Talk about the ultimate in a unique experience as well as a dramatic change in perspective. As the first man to walk on the moon, Neil Armstrong's evocative description of what it's like to see the earth from outer space really gets you thinking. Don't differences among people, nations, races, creeds, or religions assume a different level of importance? Don't personal troubles that seem significant in the moment change their character when viewed from millions of miles away?*

Mostly, for me, Armstrong's observation gets me thinking about what some people call the neutral observer, our ability to see things without judgment/from a distance. Setting aside any emotions that really trigger you, and perhaps adding in what might be another person's perspective, what do you notice is really going on about a particular situation?

Think about it for a minute.

What's a specific conflict or difference of opinion that's currently bugging you? What's something you're beating yourself up about? What would happen if you adopted the million-mile-away standpoint to get a better handle on what's going on, and what could you learn—about the situ-

---

* For those in the know, it turns out that the moon is actually only 238,900 miles from Earth.

ation, about yourself, or about the view of someone else—from such a nonjudgmental way of considering things?

As Neil Armstrong's observation encourages us to think about what it's like to see and understand ourselves from outside our usual way of viewing things, it reminds us of the old expression about not sweating the small stuff. And as they also say, sometimes it's mostly all small stuff.

Finally, as a side note, the quote also encourages us to think that it would be quite the wonderful experience and a literal change in how we see things to head into outer space to observe firsthand the views and images that astronaut Armstrong found so moving.

How do these ideas resonate with you, and what are one or two things this week you could do to apply the mindset of the neutral observer to a conflict or issue in your own life? And another possibility: how could you take the spirit of experimentation so responsible for helping man make initial voyages into outer space to try out new perspectives on something currently going on for you?

What's Special?

"Oh, 1994, April 27. There won't be a day like that ever again. I mean, the sky was blue, with a blueness that had never been there before."

— Desmond Tutu *(archbishop, scholar, peace advocate; from* No Future without Forgiveness*)*

What events, episodes or times in your life would you describe as the kind of day there won't ever be again? A day where the "sky was blue, with a blueness there had never been before"?

What made such a day special, and what conditions and circumstances contributed to making this event such a highlight?

April 27, 1994 marked the first time South Africans— black as well as white—were allowed to cast ballots on equal terms, as citizens of their nation. For more decades than we would like to remember, the white minority had dominated all aspects of South African life, and a system of apartheid (segregation between the races) had developed and been institutionalized. The minority ruled, the majority was deprived of basic rights, and hostility and even violence were often the order of the day.

A variety of circumstances—efforts of people inside south Africa, worldwide pressure throughout the 1980s and 1990s, and the courage of African leaders, most famously Nelson Mandela who was, of course, jailed for the better part of three decades—contributed to the overdue demise of the system.

But April 27, 1994 marked not just the ending of the old but more importantly the dawn of a new era altogether.

In addition to celebrating the end of apartheid, the right to vote, which is the bottom line symbol of equality in a democracy, was being extended to all on an equal footing.

What an affirmative end to a long journey, and no wonder Archbishop Tutu, himself an activist in the struggle, was moved to write with such evocative imagery. He reminds us to consider the impact of important events too easily put on the historical back burner.

At the same time, I think a man of such enormous humanity would be pleased, without trivializing the momentous historical event he was recounting, to see us adapt his ideas and apply them at a more personal level. He'd want each of us to follow our individual dreams to make our own sky as blue as it can be, he'd encourage us to put more "special" out into the world, and he'd be happy that by doing so, each of us would be playing our own little part toward making the world a little bit better of a place.

How do these ideas resonate with you, and in what one or two ways this week might you use these thoughts to make the blue sky of your life just a little bit bluer?

Fullness

"Without black, no color has any depth. But if you mix black with everything, suddenly there's shadow—no, not just shadow, but fullness. You've got to be willing to mix black into your palette if you want to create something that's real."

– Amy Grant (singer/songwriter)

Not always easy or happy questions, but what have you taken away from some "down" times in your life? Some "negative" experiences or even extended "dark" periods?

No, of course I'm not suggesting that we all head outside to find a disappointment or a frustration. I'm not asking you to see things from a perspective of half empty.

Quite the opposite—anything we can do to minimize the down side is probably a good thing.

I do, however, like Amy Grant's quote because it's a reminder to see the "dark side" as something we can truly learn from. It's so natural to want to put a good face on negative experiences, to block out the painful feelings, or even to deny that a bad thing has happened.

What if instead, we acknowledge the "shadow," allowing the "darkness" to add to the depth and wonder of life? What if we took time to learn from those experiences that didn't work out to understand how to be more successful, and what if we changed the perspective in the first place away from concepts of "dark" and "light" to see, as Amy Grant does, the possibility for more overall fullness? Finally, what if, as she suggests, we just took more time to get real?

How do these ideas resonate with you, how this week did you deal with a frustrating situation, and in what one or two ways might you use Amy Grant's observation to better a specific circumstance in your life?

Truth

"Blueness doth express Trueness."

– Ben Johnson (playwright)

What's true for you? What's most important? In the present moment? As you think about things coming up a little down the road? When you reflect on the really big kinds of questions that color your life?

Wow, sometimes it sure is easier to answer these big questions one step at a time and to break them down with reference to a specific focus that matters to you.

But even in small ways, do you remember to take time to ask about what's most important or really "true" for you?

The quote above is so simple; at the same time, it's so profound. As the color often associated with qualities including loyalty, serenity, and calm, blue points us in a direction of focusing inward. It reminds us to put first things first, and it asks us to move toward the heart of the process of getting in touch with ourselves and becoming clearer about what's really inside.

And once you're in that still small place, how much easier is it to get in sync with what resonates or strikes you as most real?

It also can be true that really big ideas, such as those about one's fundamental purpose in life, can be just too darned big.

Sometimes it's easier—at least for me—to get to a "big" thing by taking a series of smaller steps; sometimes I have no particular plan in mind when simply starting a journey.

How do these ideas resonate with you? In what one or two ways this week, big or small, might you use Ben Johnson's short but on-the-mark observation to go a little deeper inside and to get just a little clearer about some things really important to you or to get a little closer to what's true for you?

Experience

"The sky grew darker, painted blue on blue, one stroke at a time, into deeper and deeper shades of night."

– Haruki Murakami, *(author, from* Dance Dance Dance*)*

In what ways this week have you gone deep into an experience? You watched what you thought was an interesting interaction looking out your window, and you kept wondering what the participants were up to. You had a really good meal, and you kept thinking about all the ways it was enjoyable. You had a meaningful conversation, and you were moved to deepen your reflection as to what you learned.

On the other hand, in what ways have you noticed yourself quickly letting a potentially significant experience go? You turned away from what looked to be an intriguing interaction on the street. You had a good meal, and you didn't take time to consider what you liked about it. There was an important conversation, and you simply moved on to your next appointment. You perhaps had an intuition there might be more to notice, and yet you didn't follow through to give it the thought or the feeling or the time you had an instinct it deserved.

Isn't that latter way of being such a natural tendency?

And at the same time, what a wonderfully evocative reminder Haruki Murakami provides by highlighting that there just might be a different way. He's encouraging us to slow down to become a keener observer, and in so doing, he wants each of us to really get the most out of each and every experience. His imagery invoking the darkening of the night sky is all the more powerful because the activity of observing that sky is so simple and so universal. Each day each of us has the opportunity to head outside and look upward as night approaches. How often do we take advantage of the moment? How much patience do we have to keep observing, and how much time do we take to notice and process the rich changes in color Murakami describes?

What would it be like to apply this mode of being to situations and activities which are more personal?

It's not always easy to stay so patient, so observant, or so focused. And yet how rich are the rewards! Rewards including processing experiences so we can make the next ones more successful. Slowing ourselves down so we can stay longer in a calmer place. Enhancing our powers of observation. And just appreciating moment by moment the positive things in our lives.

How do these ideas resonate with you? And how this week might you want to, even for a few minutes, find one or two ways to go deeper into an experience, making it more special in the process?

Do the Work!

"I write in longhand on yellow legal pads."

    – *Beverly Cleary* (*author,* Henry Huggins *and* Ramona *series*)

You have a goal, a dream, something you really, really want? What do you do about it? Creatively imagine possibilities? Read everything you can about the topic? Talk to friends? Do nothing? Actually all really good strategies, and sometimes even "doing nothing" is not a bad thing. You say you want to go further, but sometimes it's enough to brainstorm a little and to just have fun hashing out some project that's not ever meant to come to fruition.

But for the dreams you truly desire to see come true, how do you feel about getting down to the real nitty gritty and doing the work? Is it too hard? Too scary? Too many steps involved?

There's a lot of talk these days about the so-called Law of Attraction: your attitude on the inside impacts the chance you will be able to manifest your dream out there in the world. As personal growth guru Napoleon Hill profoundly wrote as the title for his famous book, *Think and Grow Rich.*

And there's a lot of truth to these ideas: cultivating imagination and a positive attitude counts for a lot.

But author Beverly Cleary's quote highlights for me an often overlooked piece of the picture; at the same time as it's crucial to dream and to stay positive, it's still equally important to just do the work. Her symbolism of writing in long hand on yellow legal pads reinforces the idea of just getting down to business. Isn't that a nice metaphor, especially in the age of the modern day computer, to remind us to simply roll up our sleeves to take care of what needs to be done?

And what about the related possibility that rather than representing some kind of tiresome drudgery you don't want to slog through, the work on those yellow legal pads could actually be viewed in a positive light? It can help you generate ideas, develop discipline, and even get you moving forward. As such, it can become an equally important part of the process of turning your dreams into reality.

There's no doubt your excitement about the goals and dreams you have set for yourself, as well as cultivating a positive attitude, will carry you a long way. Such a mindset will make things easier, and it'll keep you motivated. Don't forget though that it's the yellow legal pads that will take your dreams to the next level of your desire.

How do these ideas resonate with you, and how might sitting with one or two of those literal or metaphorical yellow legal pads this week move at least one dream of yours a step or two closer to coming true?

Decisions

"And as a director, you make 1000 decisions a day, mostly binary decisions: yes or no, this one or that one, the red one or the blue one, faster or slower. And it's the culmination of those decisions that define the tone of the film and whether or not it moves people."

— Jason Reitman (film director)

How many decisions have you made over the last couple of days? Over the last couple of hours? About what, and with what level of difficulty? How much thought have you given to the idea that you're even making decisions at all?

Jason Reitman reminds us that even if we're not film directors, we make decisions more often than we think. Decisions, decisions, everywhere, decisions. For the moment setting aside the big ones—career or relationship choices—we make small ones all the time. To take a walk or to stay home. To bring lunch to work or to buy from the cafeteria. To call a friend or to leave communication until later. Even a failure to decide something is of course really a choice in itself.

And yet, Reitman is also correct that the sum total of these choices, decisions, and actions affect the tone and quality of our lives as well as, as he reminds us, our ability to move people.

I don't know if I agree with him that so many of our decisions are indeed binary. Do we, as he suggests, generally see ourselves as choosing between two opposing options: for instance, deciding between "red" or "blue," or between "yes" or "no"? Often, the number of alternatives seems to be less clear cut and additionally may change as we reflect on or engage in discussion over a particular matter. How many options do you tend to consider? How do those alternatives change over time? Taking time to consider each of these questions provides interesting food for thought in its own right and certainly adds to your understanding of your internal decision-making processes.

But for starters, an awful lot can be gained by recognizing the main point film director Reitman wants to get across. Begin by considering how many small decisions you make on a daily—or even an hourly—basis. What if you made your decision-making processes just a little more conscious? What if you gave yourself credit for how many actions you really take in such a short amount of time, and what if you gave yourself more pats on the back, appreciating that more of your choices work out in good ways than you realize?

In short, the simple choice of whether to wear blue or red sometime this week might be more consequential than you know.

How do these ideas resonate with you, which color (red or blue) do you usually choose, and in what one or two ways this week might you use a metaphor about your color choices to take a stand for your decisions more generally?

Spice

"Painters use red like spice."

– Derek Jarman (film director)

What do you do to add spice? How do you "spice" up the food you're cooking or the outfits you wear? In what ways do you add little touches that give more life to your projects, your activities, or even how you practice your spirituality? To what extent do you take time to brighten things up, to put your unique stamp on what's going on for you, or to inject just a small amount of physical or metaphorical color?

Derek Jarman's insight taken as a description about the process of painting is interesting in itself because it suggests one important way in which artists invoke the color red, sparingly and as an accent to enhance the look of other colors. Nice roles for red to play: as a supporter, as a brightener, and as an enhancer. Roles a little different from the way we usually think about red, as simply being a bright color attracting attention in its own right and as evocative of passion.

The reference to the cooking process deepens the analogy. How often do you add spices to what you're preparing, and which kinds? Do the ingredients you add suggest you want more salt, or do you use them to sweeten the pot? Do you stick to tried-and-true staples, or do you seek out more exotic tastes? While spices come in all flavors and varieties, the important thing is that it only takes a small amount of most to make a big difference in how the overall meal will taste.

And that's the bigger point, to use the color red as a reminder to take the time and put in the effort to add in those little touches that can truly brighten things up.

How do these ideas resonate with you? In what one or two ways this week have you taken the initiative to add spice and style to augment the quality of your activities, and how might you more generally engage in a couple of actions to add, as the saying goes, just a little more spice to your life?

Passion

"I love red so much that I almost want to paint everything red."

– Alexander Calder (artist)

Where's your passion? What really gets your juices flowing? What do you find so stimulating you just want more?

Alexander Calder's enthusiasm is uplifting and contagious, so let's follow his example to focus our own attention on the things we ourselves really care about. It's easy to get distracted. It's easy to overthink things, and it's easy to find reasons to go in multiple directions. But as we get a little lost in those twists and turns, here's a reminder that it only takes a few simple questions to get back on track. What gets you in a positive space? What makes you happy? What do you really love?

The message to focus on your passion comes across even more clearly because it happens to be the color red that makes Alexander Calder feel so good. He's chosen a color associated with a wide variety of emotions, ranging all the way from the heat of burning anger to the euphoria of deep and abiding love. As befits the idea of true passion, a lot of feelings, all of them strongly held, get linked with the color red.

In a different vein, for those familiar with the lingo of the chakras, red is also the color associated with one's personal foundation. As such, it helps you ground, center, and find support. It goes without saying that the stronger one's roots and connections to what's most fundamental, the more clarity and certainty with which one's purpose can be fulfilled/passions developed.

Finally, the color red simply grabs your attention, forcing you to engage with what it wants to say.

And in this case, as represented by Alexander Calder's enthusiasm, what red wants you to put front and center is to find the things that really keep you energized.

Doesn't Mr. Calder get you, as he did me, thinking about the things that you really love? Doesn't he do so in a really vivid way? Doesn't his excitement, which might lead him to paint not only everything, but for all we know everyone, red, get your attention?

How do these ideas resonate with you, what are some of your own passions, and what one or two specific actions might you take this week to bring a little more of them into your life?

Expanding the Choice Pie

"She turned back to inspect a bank of greens: olive, jade, leaf, kiwi, lime, a silver-green like the back of birch leaves, a bright pistachio."

– Anne Bartlett (*author, from* Knitting)

Which would you choose? A darker green like olive or a lighter shade such as lime or pistachio? Would you prefer to combine several shades, or stick to a solid color? Since Ms. Bartlett is writing about knitting, what would be your choice of texture or type of material? Would you want to make something solely green, or would you like to add in other colors?

Oops, there seems to be more complexity to what appeared to be a relatively simple choice. A knitter is faced with the—happy—task of picking one of several beautiful colors for her/his project. But where does the choice of this color fit into the broader scope of the work? What's the larger vision? Perhaps the knitter's goal is to knit a basic solid color scarf. Then the choice is indeed simply one of deciding between alternative shades. Perhaps the knitter instead wants to use the green to fit into a larger tapestry with which to decorate a room? What then?

Obviously, the kinds of questions we're asking about choosing colors for a knitting project generalize to questions about the way we make choices and decisions out there in the world where we're making such choices and decisions on a daily—if not minute-by-minute—basis. Some decisions are easy. For others there's a lot to think about. What's the goal we're trying to achieve? Who else is involved? How conscious are we of the boundaries and specifics of the alternatives?

It's the surprisingly multidimensional nature of those specifics that this quote highlights. How do you expand the character of your potential options? What do you do to deepen your understanding of the choices, how do you get to the bottom line of which aspects are most important to you, and where does one relatively small decision fit into any broader context?

It can be a bit daunting and might take some practice, and yet a little bit of conscious thought can go a long way towards making your choices a whole lot better.

How do these ideas resonate with you, and what are one or two things you could do this week to break the mold of the dichotomous black-and-white kind of thinking we're so used to when we make decisions? How might you add just a little more green?

Clarity

"I have often said that I wish I had invented blue jeans: the most spectacular, the most practical, the most relaxed and nonchalant. They have expression, modesty, sex appeal, simplicity—all I hope for in my clothes."

– Yves Saint Laurent (clothing designer)

How clear are you about the things you really want? As clear about the qualities of the day-to-day choices you make as designer Yves Saint Laurent is about choosing the clothes in his wardrobe? What about other aspects of your life such as what you would like from your next vacation, from a first date, or from the kind of pet you're looking for? What about the things that at bottom even define who you are: for example, the qualities that are musts for you in determining your ideal career or life partner?

And on a very different note, how clear are you on your answer to the question: What words would you use to describe blue jeans?

Sounds easy, doesn't it? What kind of clothes do you like? What kind of vacation would make you happy? What's your perfect job? At the same time, it often takes considerably more time and effort than expected to get a handle on our true answers to these questions, and sometimes we don't even think to ask them in the first place.

I like Yves Saint Laurent's quote because it highlights the importance of simply getting clear. Pay attention to the detail with which he describes the qualities of the clothes he desires for his wardrobe. Characteristics including expression, modesty, sex appeal, and simplicity. Hey, good for him for adding in the sex appeal part.

And not for nothing, he has also put forward a detailed vision of what he wants, and he can articulate that vision with some eloquence. He focuses on the general attributes he desires; he can then measure particular outfits according to how well they match his criteria. Elaborating on general standards has the advantage of helping him put the specifics into a broader context. And it is widely thought that the clearer you are, the higher the likelihood you'll achieve your goals.

Good for him for getting clear on broad characteristics, good for him for reminding us that wardrobe can be important, and good for him for simply liking blue jeans!

How do these ideas resonate with you, and even starting small, how this week might you get a little clearer on something you want? In what one or two ways might you test out the proposition that clarity breeds enhanced success?

Be Bold!

"The world is exploding in emerald, sage, and lusty chartreuse—neon green with so much yellow in it. It is an explosive green that, if one could watch it moment by moment throughout the day, it would grow in every dimension."

> – Amy Seidl (*author, from* Early Spring: An Ecologist and Her Children Wake to a Warming World)

What have you done today to be bold? To put yourself out there, to go against the grain, or in some way to let yourself stand out? Perhaps that kind of boldness isn't your style but then how, even in a quiet way, have you truly acted to genuinely express yourself?

The "explosive" emerald, sage, and especially chartreuse that Amy Seidl describes serve as reminders to grow, to step out courageously, and to be who you genuinely are.

You might want to start from within; and you might want to, as Amy Seidl suggests, view your own development as akin to the unfolding of the processes taking place out there in the natural world. There's already so much wonderful green, and it presents itself in objects of so many shapes, so many sizes, and of course, so many shades. It starts out pretty vibrant in the first place, and it only gets better from there. The colors and the textures keep changing, and "if one could watch it moment by moment throughout the day, it would grow [and deepen] in every dimension."

Oh, if we could only think of ourselves in such positive terms more often.

And then there's the putting yourself out there part. There's the emerald, the sage, and particularly the chartreuse—neon-bright and explosive. After all, chartreuse is such a unique color, serving to draw attention and to provide contrast to its surroundings. So therein is the reminder to follow the lead of chartreuse; it's about being you, and as you're moved to do, it's about boldly doing so.

For Amy Seidl, the chartreuse color is incredibly positive; for others, it's not a favorite. Regardless, notice. Appreciate. Learn. Let chartreuse set the example, and take a cue to stand out as you really are.

How do these ideas resonate with you? In what one or two ways this week might you choose to "explode" into a little more chartreuse or just take a couple of small steps to put more of your genuine self out there into the universe?

42. Orange, Green and Turquoise
Quote of the Week

Teaching by Example

"During summer or charity games I'll wear my bright orange or green or turquoise ones and guys are always like, 'Why are your shoes so bright?'"

— James Harden (basketball player)

In what ways this week have you been a teacher? Spent time showing someone how to do something? Set some kind of example? What does it mean to you to "teach," and do you even think of yourself as someone acting in this capacity?

A good teacher can show up in a wide variety of unexpected places. Of course there's the formal classroom where there's specific material to be covered. There's also a wide range of community forums (churches, neighborhood associations, etc.) where the purpose may not be to deliver specific content but to learn and to work through discussion and the dynamics of the group process.

Then there's the informal teaching and learning—sometimes deliberate, sometimes less consciously planned—that occurs simply by taking who you really are out there into the world.

Enter—or should we say run—into this world of informal teaching: basketball player James Harden. People expect him to wear one sort of shoe—the kind everyone else wears—and he comes in with something different: bright colored and easily noticeable shoes. He clearly wants to stand out and to get people's attention, and he's choosing to do it in a way he doesn't even need to articulate. He simply needs to step out there on the court and do what he's so good at—play ball.

But with this simple act, there's the potential for Harden to do a whole lot of educating. He can show donors at charity games that basketball players don't always fit the stereotypes with which they're often tagged. He can show youngsters—some of whom may be lacking in both opportunities and role models—that it's okay to try something a little outside the box. Perhaps wearing different shoes even provides reinforcement for Harden himself to remember the values and principles most important to him.

Even a small act of setting an example has the potential to make a big difference.

How do these ideas resonate with you? How this week have you acted as a teacher, and if you want to, what are one or two things you might do to consciously develop that role?

Getting Started

"I'm useless at staring at a piece of white paper. But if you put a piece of white paper with a black line on it in front of me, I'll say no that black line should be red and it should go this way or that way."

— Marc Jacobs *(clothing designer)*

How do you get started on a creative project? On making a difficult decision? On any endeavor where you're stuck and where what's in front of you looks and feels like a blank slate? You simply have no idea how or where to begin.

Sometimes this phase is the hardest part of any activity. There's no clarity about the goal, the options, the solutions, or even the overall vision. It's the ambiguity of being at the beginning that can keep important ideas from ever getting off the ground.

So what do you do when you're stuck? Just get mad? Give up? Feel hopeless? Mark Jacobs' description is inspiring because he shows us there's another—and better—way. In addition to validating that even wildly successful people have their share of difficulty—not an unimportant point for us to hear—he's really emphasizing a process of trial and error that gets results for him. What works? What doesn't?

What can you yourself do to develop a system that's effective for you?

Designer Jacobs doesn't get anywhere just staring at a blank slate, waiting for ideas to come. But he doesn't just give up either.

He's really good at reacting to something that's already on paper or which has been brought to him by someone else. Get something down—anything. What does it look like?

How do you like it? What would you change? What can you do to make it just a little better?

This is a great lesson about thinking more consciously about the processes that help you when you're staring miserably at some metaphorical blank slate, and it's downright inspirational to know how possible it is to find ways to break through.

How do these ideas resonate with you, and what are one or two new approaches you could try this week to help you move forward from a place you're stuck?

Learning

"Learning operatic roles is ongoing, and I find that I can learn on the train or subway, during a manicure, getting my hair done, and even while driving if I only look at the score at red lights."

– *Renee Fleming (opera singer)*

Where and how do you do your learning? In formal classrooms? In your interactions with other people? In any given day, do you even think about how much you have actually learned?

Renee Fleming's description reminds us that there's more learning going on, on a daily basis and in places we never thought were possible. The type of information processing an opera singer is expected to engage in is to the outsider pretty mind-blowing. Just think about all the necessary activities: memorize words and music in several languages, develop some pretty consummate acting skills, and put everything together into a wonderful performance. Not to mention the people savvy necessary to deal with your potentially adoring fans as well as temperamental coworkers. You'd think Renee Fleming—as well as all other opera singers—would be hanging out in their ivory towers with little time to have a life.

Apparently, quite the opposite.

Fleming's description is so inspiring because, acknowledging the skill level of her work, she's breaking the things she needs to study into bits and pieces, and she's fitting her times for learning into the ordinary activities that make up her life. While she's on trains and subways; during her manicures; even when she's stopped in traffic at red lights. Hmm, I hope she's making some quick transitions as the light changes!

She's certainly debunking stereotypes about the lives of opera singers, and more importantly, she's teaching us a lot about all the unexpected options and choices we ourselves have about where and how to learn. Inadvertently too, she's linking the desire to learn with a warm and happy color, providing even more encouragement to engage in the learning process.

How do these ideas resonate with you, in what one or two ways this week have you learned more than you thought, and what are a couple of things you could do to incorporate just a little more learning into your life?

The Unknown

"Everything changes when a man becomes purple."

– Charlie McDonnell (musician, comedian)

Hmm, what do you think he means by this? What does it mean to become purple? Is it about wearing purple clothing or painting your face? Your entire skin? Is it walking around with a certain type of attitude or personality characteristic? If men can become purple, can women do it too?

And how does the process unfold? Do you wake up one morning and just find that you've turned purple? Do you have to work at the change, and if so, what skills are required?

Sounds intriguing, doesn't it? And actually kind of fun!

Wouldn't it be nice if we could approach all the unknowns and difficult questions out there in the big wide world with this same kind of attitude of anticipation and curiosity?

How are we going to get all of our work done? What's our next career move? What's our life purpose anyway?

Whew, the questions are getting harder. Can't you start to feel a similar change in the atmosphere? Notice yourself getting anxious? Uncomfortable?

But what if we could, when faced with questions for which we don't yet have answers or situations we can't anticipate, adopt the attitude of someone who might have just turned—or been turned—purple? What fun is to be had? What's it going to be like? Hey, I'm purple. I'm curious. I've got the skills and resources to deal with whatever happens, and I trust things will work out.

How do these ideas resonate with you, how in this spirit can you bring a little more purple into your life, and in what one or two ways this week might you use this additional color to put any uncertainties and unknowns in a bit of a different perspective?

Desire

"If I keep a green bough in my heart, the singing bird will come."

– Chinese Proverb

What do you really want? What does your heart desire? What's in your heart now, and what's the green bough that will open up more possibilities?

This Chinese proverb offers up a lovely image, and there's some pretty good food for thought here too.

What exactly does it mean to keep a green bough in your heart? Does it mean to get clear on what you desire and then keep a focus on that which you truly wish? Does it emphasize that if you really believe in the abundance of the possibilities, you're more likely to get what you want out there in the real world? Does the green bough symbolize the importance of setting the stage for the conditions that will increase the chance your desire will come to fruition? After all, that wonderful singing bird, presumably of many colors, needs some enticement. If he sees a beautiful green bough on which to perch, don't you think he'll be more likely to call the space you're providing home?

And the singing bird himself offers us a pretty inspiring image. He's beautiful. He invokes many of our senses—of sight, of hearing, and maybe even of touch. He's out there in nature, and he's supported by a magical and changing environment. In short, he's simply intriguing, urging us to go deeper and find out more and more about him and the possibilities he holds out.

How do these ideas resonate with you, and what are one or two things you could do this week to start developing that green bough in your heart?

Days Like This!

"Invention flags, his brain goes muddy, and black despair succeeds brown study."

— *William Congreve (playwright)*

We've all had days like this, right? You start off great. You're on a roll. Everything's working out just the way you planned, and you're just about on top of the world.

Oops, suddenly, something happens. Things start going wrong or not quite the way you thought they were supposed to.

You get set off.

Invention not only flags, but you're starting to feel out of control. Other things may go wrong too, and by the time it's all said and done, life itself seems to spiral from bad to worse.

The day that started off filled with so much promise has somehow—sometimes we don't even understand how—been transformed, only to end up in a brown study. Even a black despair you feel will never lift?

How do you turn things around?

At these times, it's probably useful to consider what you can do to switch gears, and just recognizing that there are indeed strategies out there to get out of a situation that seems hopeless can be a big help in itself. Actually, if you think about it, there are more ways to do this than you might initially expect. Spend half an hour—or more—hitting a punching bag and screaming? Take some deep breaths and sort out what you have learned? Smile at something even as simple as Congreve's comedic quote? What else works for you?

But it's also the case that a prior first step, if not always an easy one, may be to take some time to simply stick with and feel the unhappy and out-of-control feelings. You're frustrated, you're pissed off, and you're overwhelmed. Bad days happen even to good people, and a bad day today certainly doesn't preclude a better outcome tomorrow. There's no particular need to seek out "brown study" or "black despair," and yet, learning to move through those feelings reflects a natural and normal part of life.

And hey, it can't be all bad because these are also pretty colorful phrases.

How do these ideas resonate with you, in what one or two ways this week might you honor some of the "brown" and "black" feelings that have come to you, and in what ways might (or might not) that process move you forward?

Dialogue

"From the political angle, I'm trying to be apolitical if you will. I mean people say, 'Are you a red state or blue state?', I say, 'I'm purple.' I think there are great ideas on both sides of the aisle and neither side has cornered the market."

– Brad Thor (novelist)

What do you think of Mr. Thor's ideas? We can learn from viewpoints and opinions from people on all sides of the spectrum? Of all the possibilities out there involving politics, as well as just about any other context, we might take from any source to choose ideas and solutions which make for the best?

I bet you're expressing a resounding yes to these questions, and on the other hand I bet if you give it a little more thought, and if you're like me, you don't always stretch out in this way? Isn't it easy to get stuck in your own beliefs or to hang out only with people who take your side? To hesitate to interact with people who are "different" from you?

But what exactly constitutes "different"? What are the dimensions and to what degree? What's the venue for hanging out: a community forum to discuss an issue, a political party event, or a discussion over your own dinner table? How important is the issue/concern to you, and what people/sources might influence your thinking?

Mr. Thor refers to political and partisan dialog and the often-invoked red-state (Republican) / blue-state (Democrat) distinction. What about more personal contexts? How do you deal with differences at home, among friends, or with people in the larger community; and in what ways might you capitalize on these differences to actually develop more win-wins? How does the source of an idea impact your thinking?

One final point: As Mr. Thor says, there are good ideas emanating from people in both red and blue states. But what happens when you combine those colors?

Purple not only brings the best of both worlds, but it's also an important color in its own right, with characteristics very different than those of its component red and blue parts. Once you take time to consider the best of the best, you have come up with something pretty wonderful and unique.

How do these ideas resonate with you, and if you want to, in what one or two ways this week might you stretch out to generate a little more "purple" in your thinking?

Noticing

"I think the more yellows, the more lights, the better. It alerts everybody. I mean, I guess I'm always a little bit afraid when the yellow comes out, we all get out of it, that someone won't notice it, pile into the back of you."

— Danica Patrick (racecar driver)

In what ways do you pay attention to the environment around you? What kinds of things do you notice? How do you react to what you see?

Danica Patrick's observations provide an unusually critical example of the consequences of what you do or don't observe. On a racecar track, being on top of what's going on is key. Split second reactions to situations are a necessity, and in worst case scenarios, they can literally impact life or death.

But let's not undervalue the importance of paying attention in more day-to-day situations too. The possibilities for things we might notice are endless. What are people wearing? Are they looking happy? Are they talking to each other or just hanging out? What might they be thinking? Does anyone look like they need a hug?

As she's afraid people won't see and will pile into each other, Danica Patrick raises the reverse possibility too: What are the consequences of not noticing? What important thing might we be missing? How might observing more closely better serve us?

You get the idea that paying attention matters. You're better off if you do, and you might miss something important if you don't.

So even without the yellow lights on a race track, let's take a few minutes to get out of the bubbles we so easily get stuck in, and let's take some time to do the thing we were taught to do back in grammar school—stop, look, and listen to what's around us. Maybe, just maybe, it'll lead us to finding some new and different kind of light.

How do these ideas resonate with you, and what one or two things might you do this week to incorporate a little more noticing in your life?

Good Times

"We would load up the yellow Cutlass Supreme station wagon and pick blackberries during blackberry season or spring onions during spring onion season. For us, food was part of the fabric of our day."

– Mario Batali *(chef)*

What couple of experiences come to mind when you think for a minute about events that have truly left their imprint on you? Don't make it hard or overthink it. Just what couple of instances do you recall, and what qualities have made them important?

For Mario Batali, it wasn't so much a single event that made a difference; it began with repeated family excursions, and his quote really gives us a sense of how much those times meant to him. There's his memories of loading the car, his vivid recall of its bright yellow color and make, and the goodies (blackberries and onions) the family would bring home. There's the excitement of preparing for a trip, the camaraderie, and even the simple bonding over food.

At a deeper level, there's the way "food was a part of the fabric" of the day, and you can feel the strength of the family unit when he describes things in terms of "us" and "our." For him, there's no holding back on the love and community he so treasures.

It seems fitting that the color of the family car so well remembered by Mr. Batali was a warm, happy yellow.

And given his comments, it seems not only appropriate but also actually a wonderful testament to his background that he would later become a well-known and well respected chef.

In addition, in a way that probably would make him happy, Mr. Batali's reminiscences provide for the rest of us "food" of a different sort—they raise truly profound questions. What experiences have most shaped our own lives? How can Mr. Batali's vividness and warmth of description deepen our own appreciation for our happiest memories, and how might engaging in this sort of activity propel us towards our next steps along our own modern day journeys?

So in the current day, what about getting a literal or metaphorical tune-up for that bright new yellow car?

How do these ideas resonate with you, and what one or two things might you do this week to incorporate them into your life?

Metaphor

"[The colors on citrus-crate labels] went beyond nature and spoke directly to fantasy: apricot, purple, cobalt blue, sea green, cinnamon, cinnabar, mauve, yellow, orange."

– Kevin Star (professor, California historian, pop culture enthusiast)

What does this description call to mind for you? We don't exactly have the context, but Kevin Starr, a professor and chronicler of the history of the state of California, certainly invokes some evocative imagery in his characterization of the labels on what might be an otherwise unremarkable set of packing crates. What's in these crates? Why are they important? And what about them caught Professor Starr's interest? Doesn't he make you curious, and doesn't he make you want to know more?

As befits the role of teacher, Professor Starr is actually challenging us to engage in some pretty significant ways of observing. How might we more consciously follow his example to invoke imagery and metaphor to describe even the ordinary things around us? How might we cultivate our imagination and take time to fantasize about what we want in even more important areas of our lives? Mostly, how might we, as Professor Starr seems able to do, practice becoming so keenly aware of what's around us that we actually in the first place develop an eye for the small and surprising detail?

Professor Starr evokes many colors here, but perhaps it's no accident that the color purple is included on those packing crate labels. Its traditional associations with big picture ideas, intuition, imagination, and heightened powers of observation seem exactly the kind of qualities Professor Starr is asking us to develop.

So let's take time to imagine and get into the world of fantasy. Let's broaden the set of images with which we describe those imaginings, and let's take the images we create to notice, enjoy, and describe the big things but also those offering the smallest detail.

How do these ideas resonate with you, and what are one or two things you could do this week to develop some fantasies about what you notice?

Disappointment

"Sorrows are like thunderclouds, in the distance they look black, over our heads scarcely gray."

      – Jean Paul (pseudonym of Johann Paul Friedrich Richter, author)

How do you handle disappointments? Difficulties? Even sorrows?

Happy questions with easy answers, right? Well, perhaps not easy or happy at that but important nonetheless; I like this quote because it helps set disappointment in a different perspective. Things aren't as bad as they seem. When you get right down to it, those disappointments, difficulties and sorrows, in the grander scheme of things, are "over our heads scarcely gray." The issues might be easier to sort out than we think, or they might turn out to be not as difficult as we anticipated. In terms of a long run perspective, that problem that seems so insurmountable in the moment may turn out to be a minor blip on the radar screen…well, sort of.

Jean Paul's insight also presents an interesting twist on our usual way of thinking about difficulties. What's he really saying? In the distance, sorrows seem like black thunderclouds. Once just over our head, they're scarcely gray? Shouldn't it be the other way around? When some disappointment is right there happening in the moment, isn't that when things feel blackest? Jean Paul's insight provides an interesting twist because at the same time as he is putting "sorrow" into the gray area of feelings that will pass, he's also acknowledging the uncertainty and ambiguity of the potential for disappointment. Sometimes it's the anticipation of thinking something bad is going to happen with its accompanying uncertainty that's worse than the actuality; once the negative event has occurred, we're in a better position to know how to deal with it. As he tells us, things seem blackest when we don't know exactly what we're facing. So on the one hand, Jean Paul is perhaps encouraging us to find ways to minimize the worrying we're likely to do in anticipation of a negative event, and at the same time, he's acknowledging the reality of the uncertainty and the ambiguity that may in fact precede the upset.

How do these ideas resonate with you, how this week have you viewed even a small disappointment or a situation with the potential to go negative, and in what one or two ways might Jean Paul's thoughts help you dig deeper to change your perspective?

Seeing Things

"*Blue flower, red thorns! Blue flower, red thorns! Blue flower, red thorns! Oh, this would be so much easier if I wasn't color-blind!*"

— Donkey *(from the movie,* Shrek*)*

What descriptors come to mind when you think of flowers? Thorns? Donkeys? What colors? Feelings?

For me, upon finding this quote, as friends will attest, I just kept saying "this is so funny." Here's some colorblind donkey presumably wandering through some forest trying to figure out where to step. Where's a flower, and where's a thorn? Where's a flower, and where's a thorn?

And at the same time, doesn't this quote raise some really fundamental questions about the importance of perspective and how we see or relate to things? Why for instance does Donkey describe the flowers (presumably good things) as blue and the thorns (bad things?) as red? Because someone has explained it to him? Because those are the images he has about flowers and thorns? Especially if he can't tell the difference in the first place, why does he think in terms of color at all?

The fun of it is that there are no right answers, and each of us has our own individualized response. Whether we're focusing on the colors of objects, as Donkey is as he's walking through his field, or whether we're dealing with so many other aspects of our everyday experience, isn't it great that we each have our own way to chronicle what we "see"? Ask a group of people for instance to describe the color red (or the color blue) and you'll get a wider variety of characterizations and associations than you ever would have expected.

Ask ten friends to tell you what flowers (or thorns) mean to them, and you'll also hear a myriad of answers.

Donkey makes us laugh, but he also reminds us that there are many ways to perceive and to experience.

How do these ideas resonate with you, and in what one or two ways this week might you follow Donkey's lead to head out to some literal or metaphorical field and, in your own words, describe what you see?

Experiencing

"I didn't come here with the intention of signing on the dotted line right away. I had to step off the plane and see how it felt to walk in purple and gold. And it's not bad. It's not bad at all."

– William Henderson (NFL football player)

How do you decide your next career move? Who you will ask out for a date? Whether you want to buy a house?

More generally, and this can be a hard one, what criteria do you use when you need to make a difficult choice?

Football player William Henderson (1990s-2000s) was faced with one of these pretty consequential choices when deciding his next career move. A long time star with the Green Bay Packers known for his contributions to the community as well as on the field, Henderson found himself courted by division rival—and those in the know, know it's a serious rivalry—Minnesota Vikings (the purple and gold).

What to do? How to choose? Would he make a decision based on information he received about alternative team personnel? Ask the advice of others? Go with the highest bidder?

For sure all reasonable strategies; and for sure, he must have figured all these factors in as he was determining his ultimate destination.

What resonates for me though about this description is that Mr. Henderson based his decision not only on intellectual criteria, but he also took into account his own direct experience. It wasn't a choice he could make just by some abstract weighing of pros and cons. He needed to get on a plane to personally check things out, and he needed to literally "see how it felt to walk in [rival] purple and gold."

Only after he found the experience "wasn't bad at all" was he ready to choose, a choice that (somewhat surprisingly given his description) in the end led him to remain with the Packers.

His strategy was more work in the long run, but as he learned, you never know how something feels until you try it out.

So as a first step, a comparison on paper of plusses and minuses is great. In addition, as was the case for football player Henderson, it's pretty important to see and experience for yourself. Personally check things out. Get involved. Feel what it's like. You might find, as Mr. Henderson apparently did, that an alternative failed to live up to your expectations, but you also might be surprised that an option you were less certain about turned out to be just "not bad at all."

How do these ideas resonate with you, and in what one or two ways this week might you go out of your way to incorporate some direct experience into your decision-making?

Alert?

"Be on the alert, like the red ant that moves with its claws wide open."

– Ugandan Proverb

What's your take on this quote? What does it mean to be "on the alert"? From a different perspective, how does it feel to learn from a metaphor invoking the imagery of a creature we usually think of in pretty disparaging terms?

My first response to the imagery presented in this proverb was indeed a little skeptical. What does it mean to be on the alert? To live in an on-the-alert kind of way? Here's this creature walking around. He's so small I probably won't even see him, and he moves with his claws wide open, ready to grab some poor unsuspecting bug or to come unwanted into my house.

So "on the alert" means you're always on guard? Playing defense? Ready to make sure you'll get that which is right-fully yours?

But in addition, think a little more deeply. What else could "on the alert" mean?

Curiosity? Interest? Seeking the new and heretofore un-noticed aspects of everyday situations? Searching out the unusual or looking for new adventures? Just increasing the attention you pay to what's around you?

It's so easy to go on automatic pilot, to do the same old thing, or to walk the tried-and-true routes. Maybe it's not the best idea for us humans to consistently keep our claws wide open, but what about our eyes, ears, and other senses? What about staying in the moment to enhance your powers of observation?

I'm starting, despite his open claws, to feel better and better about this creature's way of living!

And there's even one more lesson that little red ant wants to teach us. Rather than standing still and waiting for things to happen to him, in smart ways, he's consistently on the move. He's checking the terrain, He's looking for needed food, and he's searching out more and more of the good things he might run into on his adventures.

Could it be that little red ants are smarter than we think?

I can't speak directly to him to find out what he himself is really understanding about the meaning of being on the alert, but I kind of want to thank that little red ant for offering a reminder that's more powerful than he might know.

How do these ideas resonate with you, what do you think of the journey of the ant, and in what one or two ways this week might you want to take some action to be more in alignment with his "on the alert" way of living?

56. Orange, Purple and Green Quote of the Week
The Unexpected!

"It can be bright orange to dark purple to green."

– Mark Mallory (scientist/researcher, Canadian Wildlife Service)

What do you think he's talking about? What do you think captured Mr. Mallory's attention? Flowers? T-shirts? Potential colors for some new city subway line?

It must be pretty special because these are pretty vivid colors. It's not just orange; this is bright orange. It's not just purple; this is dark purple.

And it must be something happy because it's so colorful, and there's so much contrast.

He's sure got me curious.

And in a million years, you'd never guess what the actual answer is. It's pretty arcane, so get ready for the truly unusual.

It has to do with fulmars. They're birds from very northern climates, and the colors Mr. Mallory is talking about are descriptions of the vomit—you read that right: vomit—from these birds.

So much for the idea of happy colors and beautiful contrasts.

It turns out though that the birds' vomit is important because, among other things, it's their prime protection mechanism. As well, studying these particular birds matters because they help scientists understand issues about the larger food chain. "Fulmars separate oil from the squid, fish and krill they devour and store it in a muscular throat pouch. That oil is energy-rich food that can serve as a back-up fuel tank for themselves, nutrition for their young, or a means of scaring off predators like ravens, glaucous gulls, and foxes after their eggs—and even the odd biologist."*

Additionally, fulmars have been known to fly unusually long routes (some as much as five thousand miles from parts of Canada across the Atlantic to Ireland) and to sit protectively on the eggs of their unhatched young for as long as a ten-day period, even in notably poor weather.

It was noticing the unusual colors of the vomit that was among the reasons Mr. Mallory became interested in fulmars, and his dedication and commitment has led him to do much to engage in scientific exploration. He has actively traversed some pretty treacherous northern landscapes, has gone deep into the habitats of the birds, and has banded them, putting on trackers to follow their flight.

Had you asked Mr. Mallory as a young boy how he would be spending his adult years, you probably wouldn't have heard him predict that he'd become a worldwide expert studying an arcane species of bird.

But you just never know what small fact or puzzle will suddenly intrigue you, will get you curious, or will just plain catch your attention.

How do these ideas resonate with you, and in what one or two ways this week might you follow Mr. Mallory's example to get curious about something you never expected to even notice? You might even follow up on Mr. Mallory's original observation in a very different way; you might choose to forget the fulmars altogether and return to the original quote to have some fun by asking: What other things range from "bright orange to dark purple to green"?

---

* From "Nunavut's projectile pukers" by John Thompson, *Nunatsiaq Online*. http://www.nunatsiaqonline.ca/stories/article/nunavuts_projectile_pukers/

57. Orange, Green and Gold Quote of the Week

Teamwork

"He hangs in shades the orange bright / Like golden lamps in a green night."

— Andrew Marvell (British poet/politician,
from his poem "Bermudas")

As you read this, what do you think Mr. Marvell had in mind? What images or feelings come front and center as you read the line from his poem? What attracted me to this language is the colorful imagery. I thought, I don't know exactly what this means but it simply makes me appreciate the wonderful color and the diversity out there. It gets me feeling a little more curious and excited about noticing what's around.

It turns out that the poem "Bermudas," from which this line was taken, was written about a group of sailors journeying in the 1600s presumably from somewhere in Europe to the islands of Bermuda; and it turns out that the "he" who turns the orange bright into "golden lamps in a green night" is in fact in praise of God, who kept the crew safe throughout their difficult journey and who brought them at the end to a truly wonderful land.

As with all good poetry, there's the potential for many take-aways. There's the beautiful colors, particularly welcoming as they represent the culmination of a long and arduous voyage. There's the emphasis on a religious deity and all the wonders and comforts that can come from the belief in such an omnipotent being. There's the profound idea that that omnipotent being is not only at hand but also is actively working for each of us as a protector and as a provider of good.

For me, one other piece stands out too. To the extent that a deity serves as such an active protector and provider, what about the possibility for each of us in turn to more consciously take action to protect, to nurture, and to provide for each other? What if each of us in a more active way tried to become, as they say, a beacon for reaching out and doing more good things in the world?

Sometimes these kinds of admonitions can sound trite, but they're also important. Those sailors on their own must have done a lot to help and support each other and to work to ensure the safety of every person on the crew. Even as they gave thanks and enjoyed their good fortune, I hope they acknowledged their own efforts, their teamwork, and the relationships which nurtured them throughout their many months at sea.

I like the poem's imagery, and I like the spirit of individual agency that calls each of us to take an active role in building community—in turn enhancing the kind of golden light Mr. Marvell wants so much for each of us to enjoy.

How do these ideas resonate with you, and in what one or two ways this week might you be moved to take some action putting into practice your interpretation?

Like this?
Want more?

Visit

www.colorreadingprofessor.com

where you'll find:

- a blog chock full of more inspirational color quotes
- monthly free teleseminars
- opportunities to coach with me
- and much, much more!

And I'd love to get your thoughts, feedback, and reactions; just email me at sally@colorreadingprofessor.com